# DO SHEEP COUNT SHEEP?

## How Animals Sleep

ALBATROS

# DO SHEEP COUNT SHEEP?
## How Animals Sleep

Written by Petra Bartíková & Illustrated by Katarína Macurová

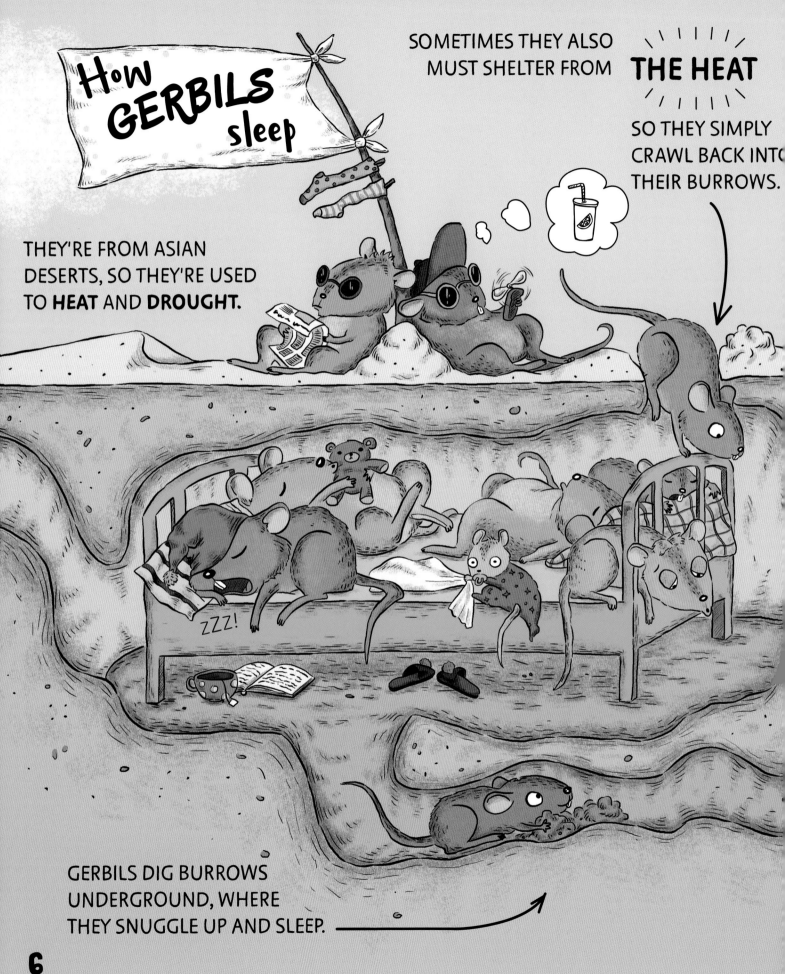

How **GERBILS** sleep

SOMETIMES THEY ALSO MUST SHELTER FROM **THE HEAT**

SO THEY SIMPLY CRAWL BACK INTO THEIR BURROWS.

THEY'RE FROM ASIAN DESERTS, SO THEY'RE USED TO **HEAT** AND **DROUGHT.**

ZZZ!

GERBILS DIG BURROWS UNDERGROUND, WHERE THEY SNUGGLE UP AND SLEEP.

# GERBILS ARE

FAST, CURIOUS, AND CUTE

## WHAT'S ALL THAT RACKET?

GERBILS ARE QUIET ANIMALS, BUT WHEN THEY START TO GNAW, SCRATCH, AND TEAR THINGS UP, THINGS GET **LOUD**!

Yum! I love grass seeds…

TICKLE TICKLE

Let´s go to bed.

GERBILS SLEEP IN THE DAY ☀ AS WELL AS AT NIGHT ◗. THEY ARE AWAKE FOR ONLY A FEW HOURS BEFORE SLEEPING AGAIN.

## GERBILS LOVE TO DIG, SQUEAK, AND

GNAW!

THEY REST
**STANDING UP**
AND EVEN CHEW LEAVES
WHILE RESTING

YUM!

ZZZ!

TO FALL ASLEEP SITTING,
THEY CURVE THEIR LONG
NECKS LIKE A PRETZEL.

## HOW LONG DO THEY SLEEP?

THEY'RE NOT BIG SLEEPERS;
ONLY A FEW MINUTES A DAY ARE ENOUGH.

# How KOALAS sleep

THESE **CUDDLY LITTLE** CREATURES WITH THICK SOFT FUR LIVE IN AUSTRALIA.

*Share some with me!*

THEY EAT ONLY EUCALYPTUS LEAVES.

LIKE KANGAROOS, KOALAS ARE MARSUPIALS. THEY HAVE POUCHES WHERE JOEYS (BABY KOALAS) DEVELOP.

WHEN THEY'RE NOT SLEEPING, THEY'RE USUALLY EATING.

KOALAS CLIMB EUCALYPTUS TREE TRUNKS AND HARDLY EVER LEAVE THEM.

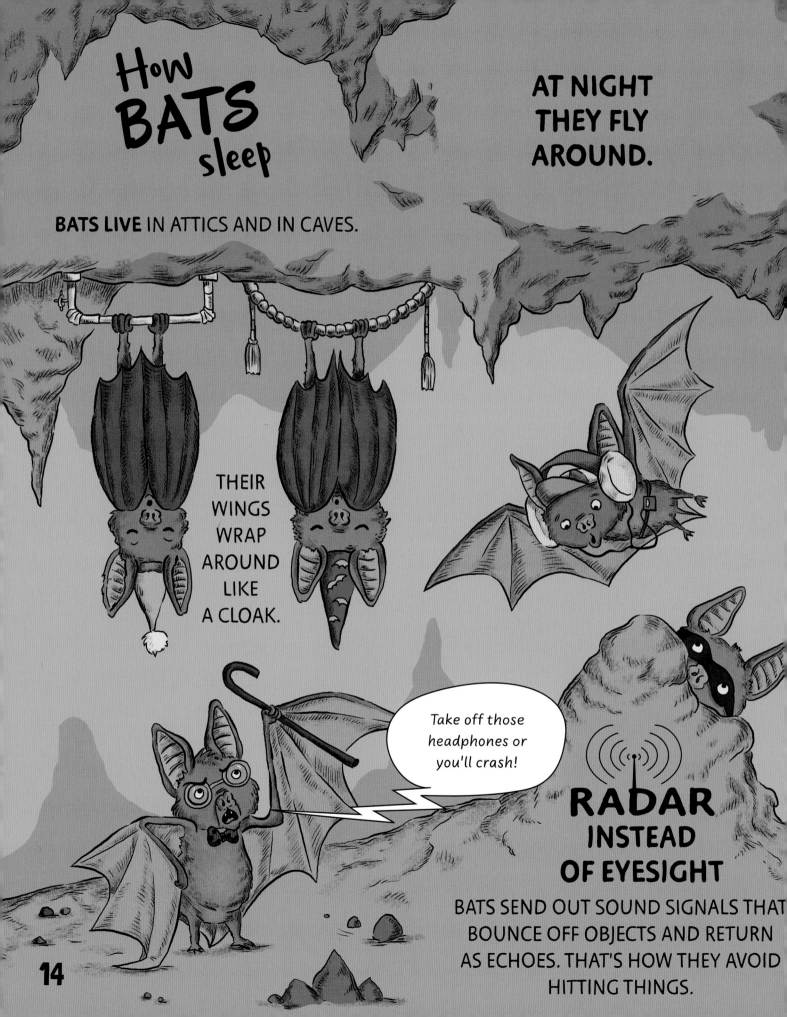

# How BATS sleep

## AT NIGHT THEY FLY AROUND.

**BATS LIVE** IN ATTICS AND IN CAVES.

THEIR WINGS WRAP AROUND LIKE A CLOAK.

Take off those headphones or you'll crash!

## RADAR INSTEAD OF EYESIGHT

BATS SEND OUT SOUND SIGNALS THAT BOUNCE OFF OBJECTS AND RETURN AS ECHOES. THAT'S HOW THEY AVOID HITTING THINGS.

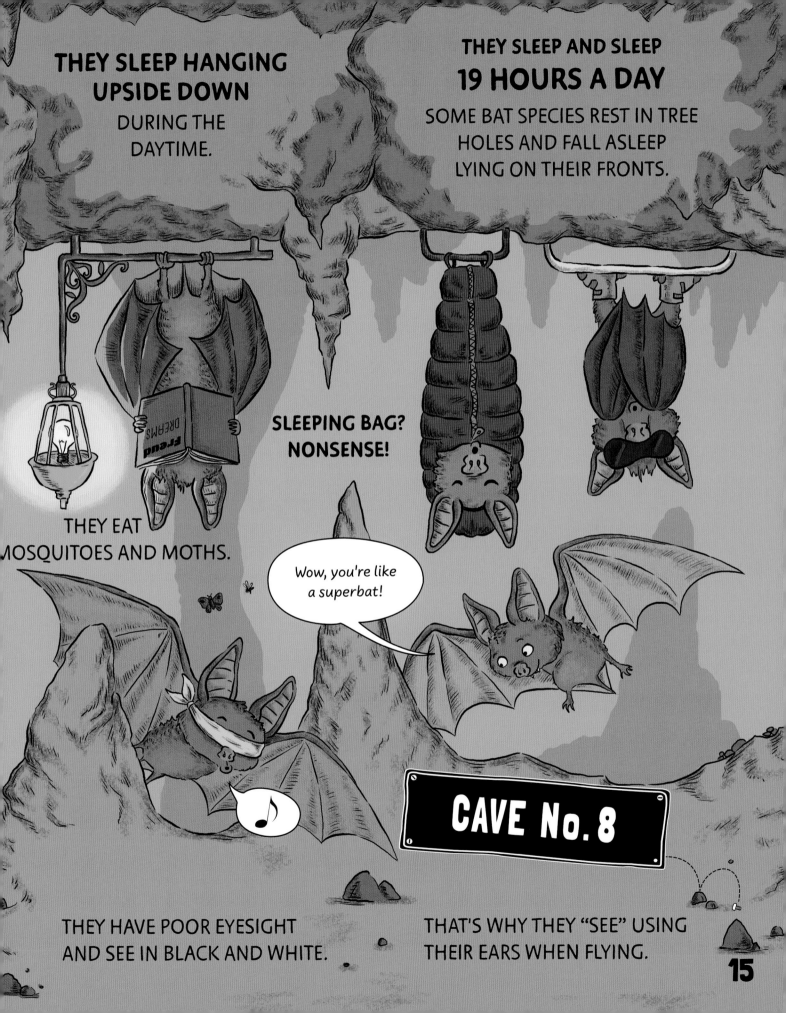

HEY, SEAL!
WHERE ARE YOUR EARS?

ON SOLID GROUND THEY ROLL...
...OR CRAWL ONTO THEIR TUMMIES.

THEIR EARS ARE HIDDEN BEHIND THEIR EYES AND ARE COVERED BY SKIN TO STOP WATER FROM GETTING IN.

IF THEY ARE NOT HUNTING, THEY JUST RELAX ON THE COAST OR IN THE PORTS.

DEEP
DEEP
UNDER
WATER

THEY CAN SLEEP UP TO 45 MINUTES STRAIGHT. WHEN THEY NEED TO TAKE A BREATH, THEY COME EASILY TO THE SURFACE.

19

THEY CAN CLIMB AND SWIM VERY WELL AND THEY RUN FAST.

HEDGEHOGS HAVE THOUSANDS OF **sharp spines** ON THEIR BODIES

WHAT IF AN ENEMY APPROACHES? HEDGEHOGS SIMPLY CURL UP INTO SPIKED ROUND BALLS, READY TO HARM ANYONE WHO BOTHERS THEM.

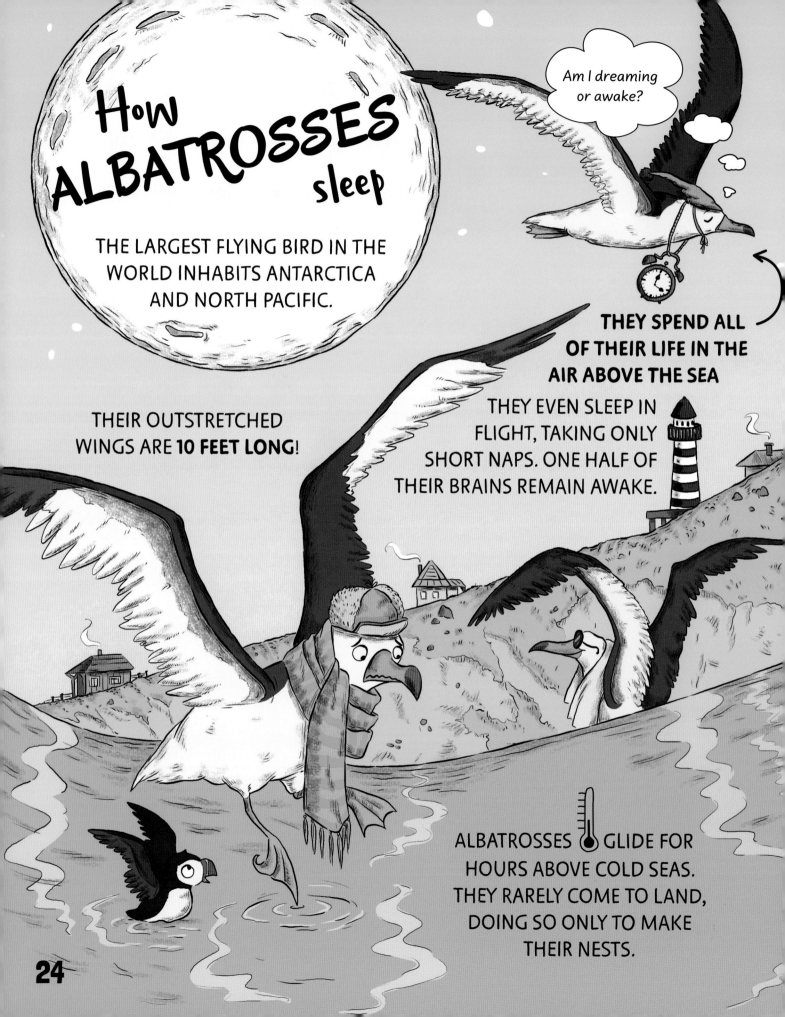

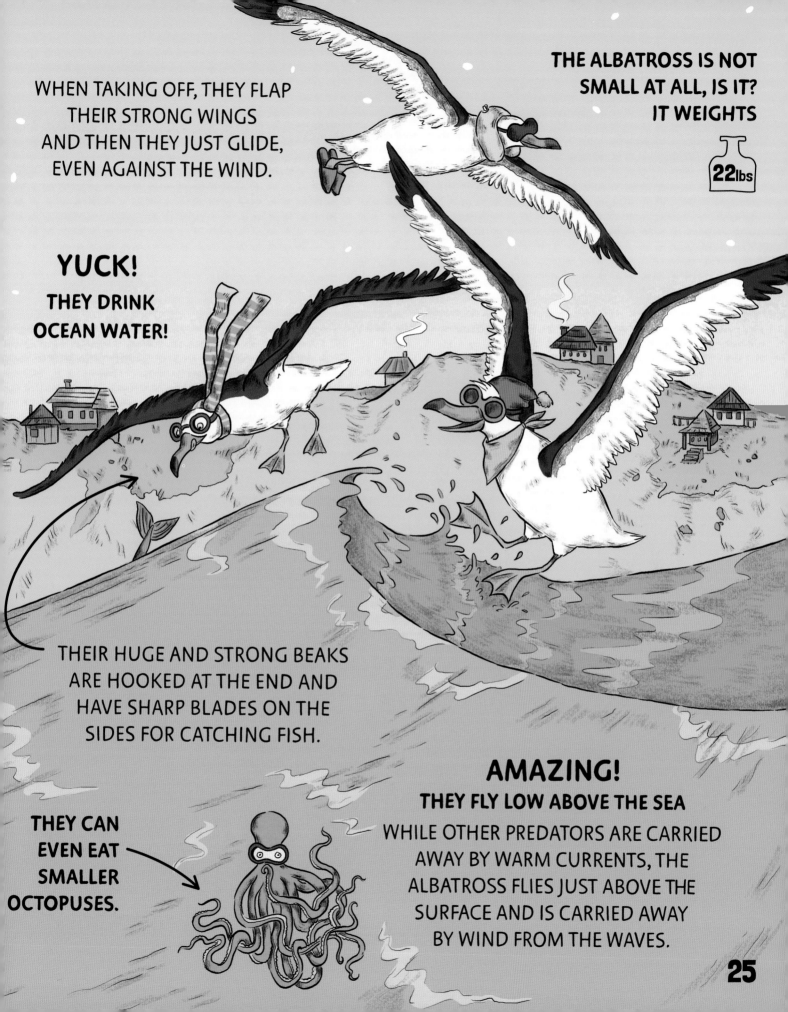

WHEN TAKING OFF, THEY FLAP THEIR STRONG WINGS AND THEN THEY JUST GLIDE, EVEN AGAINST THE WIND.

THE ALBATROSS IS NOT SMALL AT ALL, IS IT? IT WEIGHTS

**22lbs**

## YUCK!
**THEY DRINK OCEAN WATER!**

THEIR HUGE AND STRONG BEAKS ARE HOOKED AT THE END AND HAVE SHARP BLADES ON THE SIDES FOR CATCHING FISH.

**THEY CAN EVEN EAT SMALLER OCTOPUSES.**

## AMAZING!
**THEY FLY LOW ABOVE THE SEA**

WHILE OTHER PREDATORS ARE CARRIED AWAY BY WARM CURRENTS, THE ALBATROSS FLIES JUST ABOVE THE SURFACE AND IS CARRIED AWAY BY WIND FROM THE WAVES.

**25**

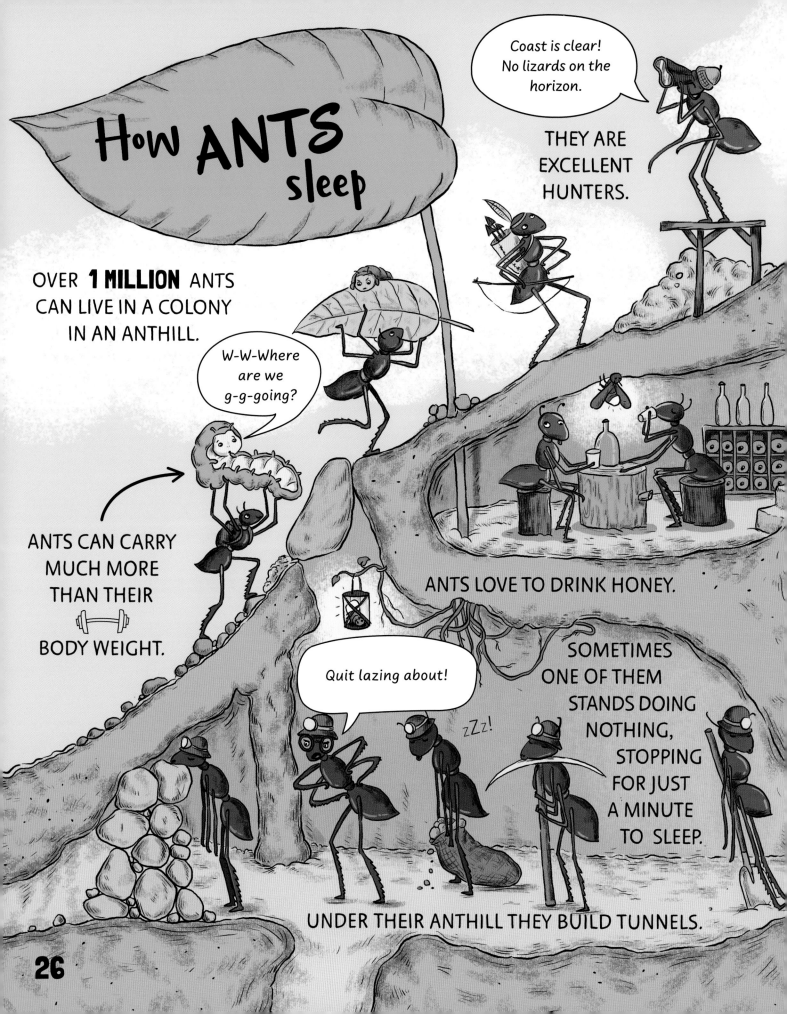

© B4U Publishing for Albatros,
an imprint of Albatros Media Group, 2024
5. května 1746/22, Prague 4, Czech Republic

Author: Petra Bartíková
Illustrator: Katarína Macurová
Editor: Scott Alexander Jones

www.albatrosbooks.com

Printed in China by Leo Paper Group.